The FREDERICK DOUGLASS
You Never Knew

BY JAMES LINCOLN COLLIER

Children's Press®
A Division of Scholastic Inc.
New York Toronto London Auckland Sydney
Mexico City New Delhi Hong Kong
Danbury, Connecticut

Library of Congress Cataloging-in-Publication Data

Collier, James Lincoln, 1928-
  The Frederick Douglass you never knew / by James Lincoln Collier;
[illustrations by Greg Copeland].
      p. cm.
Summary: Explores the childhood, character, and influential events that
shaped the life of this former slave who went on to become an abolitionist and
advisor to Abraham Lincoln.
Includes bibliographical references and index.
  ISBN 0-516-24347-0 (lib. bdg.)   0-516-25837-0 (pbk.)
  1. Douglass, Frederick, 1818-1895—Juvenile literature. 2. African American
abolitionists—Biography—Juvenile literature. 3. Abolitionists—United
States—Biography—Juvenile literature. 4. Antislavery movements—United
States—History—19th century—Juvenile literature. [1. Douglass, Frederick,
1818-1895. 2. Slaves. 3. Abolitionists. 4. Anti-slavery movements. 5. African
Americans—Biography.] I. Copeland, Greg, ill. II. Title.
  E449.D75C65 2003
  973.8'092—dc21

                              2003005251

Illustrations by Greg Copeland
Book design by A. Natacha Pimentel C.

Photographs © 2003: Art Resource, NY: 62 (National Portrait Gallery,
Smithsonian Institution, Washington, DC, U.S.A.), 25 (Reunion des Musees
Nationaux), 11 (Scala/Museum of the City of New York, New York, N.Y.,
U.S.A.); Corbis Images: cover, back cover, 1, 4, 14, 40, 65 (Bettmann), 57, 75;
Library of Congress: 69; Maryland Department, Enoch Pratt Free Library: 23,
44; North Wind Picture Archives: 7, 8, 16, 28, 37, 38, 42, 47, 53, 55, 56, 58, 66,
67, 70, 71, 72.

CONTENTS

Chapter 1
BECOMING A SLAVE

FREDERICK DOUGLASS NEVER KNEW EXACTLY when he was born, and so he never knew how old he was. He never knew who his father was. He did know his mother, but she was almost a stranger to him, for she died when he was seven, and he only saw her for a few short visits while she lived. He never went to school, and was a teenager before he could really read and write. As a child he was kept in complete ignorance of everything except the little world within a half mile of where he lived. He did not know what a city was, nor the name of the state he lived in. He did not know what a slave was, even though he was one.

Frederick Douglass at the time he was becoming celebrated

But by the time Frederick Douglass was in his twenties he was famous. In fact, one historian has said that he was the most famous black man of his time in the entire world. He would get to know several American presidents and famous people from other countries. He would give thousands of talks to countless people, not only in America but around the world. His books would be read by millions, and be translated into many languages. Indeed, they are still read today, more than a hundred and fifty years later. He was known to millions; but who was he, really?

The person we know today as Frederick Douglass was born in February 1818, as researchers have recently discovered. His mother was named Harriet Bailey, and he grew up being called Frederick Bailey. His father was almost certainly a white man. It was often whispered that his father was his master. However, he had several white masters over him; we do not know which was his father, if any of them.

He did not live with his mother. On large plantations, children were often taken from their mothers when they were little and given to an older woman to raise. This was to allow the mothers to be available to work. So Frederick was given to his mother's own mother—his grandmother—to raise.

She was Betsy Bailey. She lived with her husband, Isaac, in a rough log cabin in the woods in Talbot County, Maryland. It was then sparsely settled, with woods, river, and inlets from Chesapeake Bay.

Betsy and Isaac Bailey were luckier than most slaves. Their job was to raise the children who had been given to them until they were old enough to be put to work. Many of the children Frederick grew up with were his cousins. As long as Betsy and Isaac took good care of the children, the white master did not bother them. They had, thus, a little more independence than most slaves did.

Slaves lived in small cabins, several to a room. This cabin has a wooden floor, but many had only dirt floors.

Betsy Bailey was a strong, intelligent woman. She was an expert at growing the sweet potatoes that were an important part of the family's diet. Betsy was also an expert maker of fishing nets. She sold some of them, but she also used them to catch fish in the many rivers near the cabin.

Even so, the family was extremely poor. As a child, Frederick owned no clothes except a sort of long shirt, much like a dress, which he wore until it was in tatters. He had no shoes, much less socks, no underwear, no hat or coat. He ate his cornmeal mush with an oyster shell, because the family had no spoons.

Nonetheless, his childhood was relatively happy. If he rarely saw his mother, his grandmammy was always there. He played with his cousins in the woods or in the dust in front of the cabin or swam in the rivers. He didn't miss the toys most children have because he had never seen any and didn't know what they were.

On larger plantations, slaves lived in rows of cabins like this. Frederick would have lived with his grandmother in similar quarters at Colonel Lloyd's place, but at first he was living in a single cabin at the edge of a woods.

A few times in these years his mother appeared. She had to work during the day and could only visit at night, after a long walk. Still, she would sometimes miss a night's sleep in order to see her child, but not often. She and Frederick would talk a little, but they never grew to know each other. She died when he was still a child. He never knew exactly when she died or where she was buried. He later wrote, "I cannot say I was very deeply attached to my mother." This "terrible interference of slavery" with the natural love a child ought to have for his mother was, he afterwards felt, a great loss.

Then one day in 1824, when Frederick was six, his grandmammy took him by the hand and said they must go somewhere. She wouldn't tell him where. Off they went. On and on they walked through the summer morning. The sweat began to drip off them as the sun rose high in the sky. Twelve miles later they arrived at a strange place. All around him were great houses, far grander than anything he had ever seen. People, mostly African Americans, were at work everywhere. Children appeared, staring and laughing. Grandmammy Betsy patted Frederick on the head. "Go and play with them," she said.

But Frederick was too shy of these new children to play. So he stood with his back against the wall of a house, watching. And then, after awhile, one of the children came running up to him, shouting, "Fed, Fed! Grandmammy gone!" Frederick ran into the kitchen. Not finding her there, he rushed back outside. He looked down the road they had just come from but could not see her. His grandmother Betsy was indeed gone. She had left him to be turned into a useful slave worker on the big plantation. He had been torn away from the only family he had ever known. He fell to the ground and began to weep. He was not yet really aware of it, but he was doomed to spend the rest of his life as a slave.

In order to understand Frederick Douglass's story, we need to know something about American slavery. Slavery was not invented by Americans. There has been slavery as far back as we can go in human history. Ancient Romans and Greeks had slaves. So did many African tribes. So did other people elsewhere.

However, the situation in the Americas was particularly suited to slavery, and it was especially harsh there. Soon after settlers came to the American colonies, they discovered that much money could be made by growing tobacco in the hot climate of the South. Later on, they learned that cotton, rice, and other crops could also be grown in the South and would make the growers wealthy. Crops like these required a lot of labor. Very quickly the white settlers of Virginia, the Carolinas, and other Southern states decided to use slaves to labor in the tobacco and cotton fields. The first black slaves were brought to Virginia in 1619. Slavery spread rapidly, and by 1700 there were slaves everywhere in the British colonies that would eventually form the United States. However, most of them were in the Southern colonies.

Although we usually hear about grand plantations worked by hundreds of slaves, most slaves lived on smaller ones. This painting shows a medium-sized plantation, which probably had twenty or thirty slaves. In the background we can see the smokestacks of a Mississippi steamboat that would be carrying the cotton down the river to New Orleans, where it would be shipped to mills in the Northeast and in Europe.

By Frederick Bailey's time, slavery had mainly been abolished in the Northern states. In the South it had been well established for two hundred years. It has been called "the peculiar institution," and indeed it was. In fact, the majority of Southerners did not own any slaves. In states closest to the North, like Kentucky, there were relatively few slaves.

A fairly large minority of small farmers owned a few slaves to help with the farmwork. In these cases it took many hands to make the farm go, and the white owners had to work, too.

Finally, at the top of the heap, were a small number of large landowners who held hundreds of slaves. Some of these slaves had relatively easy jobs working as house servants, or as craftsmen shoeing horses or doing carpentry. Most of the slaves, however, worked long hours at dreadfully boring jobs, endlessly hoeing cotton or tobacco, chopping wood, shucking corn. They sweated in the Southern sun from daybreak to sundown, then went back to the slave cabins to wolf down a hasty meal of corn bread and perhaps a little pork or fish. They would catch what sleep they could on a heap of straw or even the rough dirt cabin floor. The worst of it was, they knew that this was how their lives were going to be until the day they died.

Not surprisingly, slaves worked no harder than they had to. Many lived in hope of escaping some day. Some tried; a good many actually succeeded in making their way north into the free states or Canada. But most remained to live out their toil-filled lives.

Slave owners believed that the only way to control their slaves was by fear of the lash, often a cowhide whip that could cut flesh. On the large plantations, with their hundreds of slaves, overseers rode through the fields on horseback, lash in hand, ready to strike out at a slave who appeared not to be working hard enough. Slaves who talked back, or were "impudent," might be tied up and whipped until their backs were raw and bloody. A slave who threatened a white person might be branded and whipped unconscious, and a slave who actually attacked a white was usually shot without benefit of a trial.

Not all slave owners were cruel. Some made efforts to be kind to their slaves—to see that they had enough to eat and warm clothes for cold weather. But even the kindest slave owners believed that slaves had to fear the lash.

Slave owners also believed that slaves ought to be kept in ignorance. A slave who learned to read, much less write, might start getting ideas about freedom and equality. If, for example, slaves learned that the Declaration of Independence said "all men are created equal," they might begin to wonder why they weren't free and equal. In the South it was generally against the law to teach a slave to read. Slaves who learned to read a little, as some did, had to keep well hidden the books and newspapers they managed to get hold of.

This, then, was the life that six-year-old Frederick Bailey could look forward to. He would be kept in ignorance, fed just enough cornmeal and pork to keep him strong for work, and would feel the lash on his back if he spoke out. And it was a sentence for life.

Chapter 2

GETTING AN EDUCATION

THE NEW HOME THAT FREDERICK FOUND himself in was one of those huge plantations where hundreds of slaves lived and worked. It was called Wye House. It belonged to Colonel Edward Lloyd, whose family had been in Maryland for generations. They were important people. Colonel Lloyd had been governor of Maryland, and a United States senator. He was very rich.

Slaves in a cotton field. The work was terribly hard, for the cotton pickers were bent over much of the time. As we can see, even small children were required to work long hours in the sun.

The life lived by the Lloyd family could not have been more different from the life lived by Frederick if they had come from Mars. The Lloyds did not work. Slaves did everything for them—washed their clothes, helped them dress in the morning and again every evening for dinner and the parties they often went to. Slaves cooked their lavish meals, served, and washed the dishes, while the ladies and gentlemen of the household played cards, danced, made music, gossiped. Where the slaves ate mostly cornmeal, the Lloyd family dined sumptuously on goose, quail, pheasant, oysters, crab, and trout, as well as cheese, butter, and cream from their own dairy.

A drawing of the home of a wealthy planter. Most Southern whites lived fairly rough lives on small farms with a few slaves—or none at all. But a small minority of whites with large plantations lived in great luxury. The house slaves were much envied by the field hands, for those working as cooks, housemaids, or serving boys had easier work and were usually better fed and better treated than the field hands. On Colonel Lloyd's plantation, Frederick Douglass was mainly a house slave.

Wye House was really a small town. It had its own black-smith's shop where tools were made and repaired. It had a carpenter shop for making and fixing furniture and building wagons and coaches. It had a cooperage for making barrels, a mill for grinding corn and wheat, storage barns, boats to carry its products to markets in Baltimore.

Frederick did not belong directly to Colonel Lloyd. His master was actually a man called Captain Anthony, who was the colonel's main assistant. His duty was to see that the Lloyd plantation, which was made up of several farms, ran smoothly and profitably. Captain Anthony had a big, comfortable house, although not nearly as grand as Colonel Lloyd's.

It was the custom on plantations for slaves to be given a fixed allowance of food and clothing. On Colonel Lloyd's plantation, slaves were allowed eight pounds of pork or fish, a pint of salt, and a bushel of cornmeal a month. That comes out to about a quart of meal and one meat patty a day. For clothes, each year every slave was allowed two coarse shirts, a pair of trousers, one pair of shoes and socks, and for winter, a heavier pair of trousers and a rough jacket. Needless to say, by the end of the year a slave's clothes were usually in tatters.

Frederick was soon put to work in Captain Anthony's kitchen. The kitchen was run by the cook, an African-American woman who everybody called Aunt Katy. She had children of her own, and favored them. She was particularly mean to Frederick, smacking him needlessly and sometimes refusing to give him any supper. Aunt Katy kept Frederick in misery.

Once, angry at Frederick, she gave him no breakfast and no lunch. When suppertime came he thought Aunt Katy might relent. Katy sliced off chunks of bread for her own children, but none for him. In agony he watched the other children eating merrily away, while he tried to keep from crying. But it was too much for him, and he crept outside to weep alone.

After awhile he returned and sat in a corner. Soon he noticed an ear of corn on a shelf. He slipped it down, scraped off some kernels, and put them among the embers in the fireplace to roast. They quickly cooked, and he was just about to eat this desperate little supper when into the kitchen came his mother on one of her rare visits. When she learned that Frederick had gone without food all day, she gave Aunt Katy a stern lecture. Then she pulled from her pocket a ginger cake. Frederick sat on her knee, eating the cake and feeling like "a king on his throne."

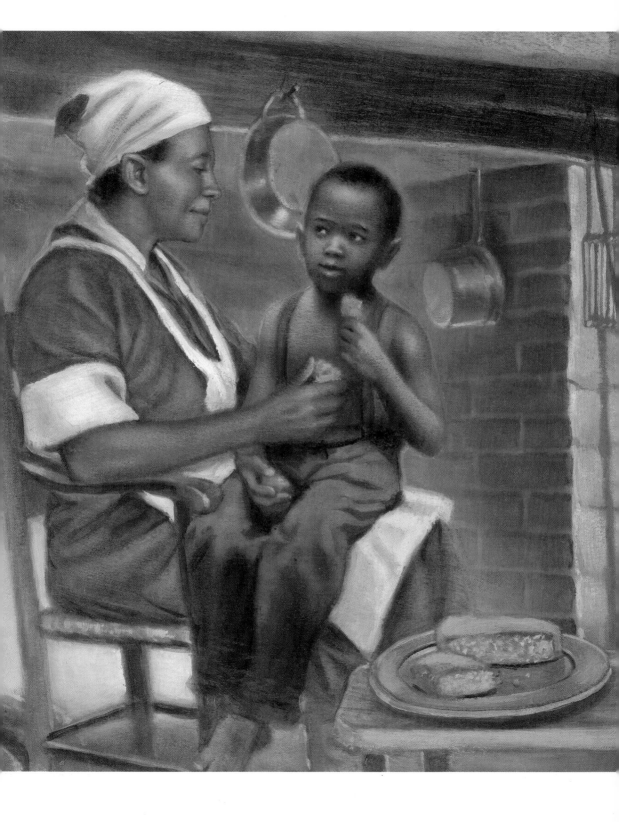

The rich and powerful Colonel Lloyd had a son named Daniel who was a few years older than Frederick. Somehow, Daniel Lloyd, who would grow up to be rich, made a friend of Frederick Bailey, a slave. In fact, in the South it was not unusual for black and white children to play together. Many times a white child living on an isolated farm might not have any other white children nearby to play with. It was often convenient for the parents to let such a child play with the slave children.

But this does not explain why Daniel Lloyd settled on Frederick, when there were many other slave children around. In fact, there was something about Frederick Bailey that attracted the attention of others, including many whites. An attraction of this sort is usually hard to explain. Partly it had to do with the fact that Frederick was very intelligent. He had a lively and curious mind. But beyond that, a sense that he was somehow special shone out of him. People were drawn to him; they wanted to help him. And this specialness would be with him all his life.

Daniel Lloyd opened doors for Frederick that might have always remained closed. He slipped him into Colonel Lloyd's great house, where he could see rooms full of fine furniture polished to a high shine, silver candlesticks gleaming, gilt-frame mirrors and pictures covering the walls, sparkling glass chandeliers hanging from the ceiling, flaming red and yellow in the sunlight.

Moreover, Daniel let Frederick sit with him while he studied with the private tutor the colonel had hired solely to educate him. From these lessons Frederick began to grasp what writing was, what a book was. He was seeing a world wholly different from the one he had been raised in. Critically important, he was coming to believe that he ought to live in that world.

It was a strange idea to enter the head of a slave. Here he was, a small boy with no education, who did not know who his father was, and barely knew his mother, who not only could not read or write, but was hopelessly ignorant of simple mathematics, of what a city was like, or even where one was, who did not know that the world was round, or what the stars were. How could such a child believe he was entitled to move into the bright and shiny world Daniel had been born into? But he believed it; and time would prove him right.

He began trying to understand that world. He asked Daniel questions. What was a senator? Who were the visitors? What was this or that fancy dish used for? Gradually his eyes opened.

Daniel Lloyd was not the only person attracted to Frederick. Another one was the daughter of his master, Lucretia Anthony Auld. She would, in time, play a very important role in his life. She was married to Thomas Auld, captain of one of Colonel Lloyd's boats. She had no children of her own. Once, Frederick got into a fight with another boy, who struck him in the forehead with something, cutting him badly. When Lucretia Auld saw the wound, she gently washed it and bound up Frederick's head. A sort of friendship sprung up between the two. Lucretia tried to protect Frederick, especially from the meanness of Aunt Katy.

In 1826 Captain Anthony was growing old and ill. Colonel Lloyd decided to hire a younger manager for his plantation. Captain Anthony had to move out of his house on the plantation. He went to one of the other farms, taking his daughter Lucretia, her husband, and the slaves.

Normally, Frederick would have gone to work on this farm as one of the field hands along with the rest of the slaves. But somehow Lucretia and her husband, Thomas Auld, wanted something better for him. Why? It is not easy to understand at this distance in time, but plainly they, too, saw in Frederick some special quality. They decided that he could not be allowed to wither in the fields.

As it happened, Thomas Auld had a brother, Hugh, who lived in Baltimore, an easy boat ride up Chesapeake Bay. Hugh Auld and his wife had a two-year-old boy. An arrangement was made for Frederick to go to live in Baltimore with Hugh Auld, in order to look after the little boy.

So off to Baltimore he went. Suddenly life for Frederick was vastly better. He had a bed instead of a bag of cornhusks. Instead of cornmeal mush for breakfast, he had good bread. Instead of a long shirt reaching to his knees for clothing, he had clean trousers and a shirt. And there was no lash. And instead of laboring long hours, his job was simply to run errands and look after the Auld's little boy, making sure that he didn't wander off or get into the streets.

Baltimore was an exciting place to be. Hugh Auld was a shipbuilder. The family lived in a section of Baltimore called Fells Point, in the harbor area. As Frederick went through the streets on errands he heard the sound of heavy hammers whanging on spikes, saws biting into wood, men shouting orders.

Baltimore harbor as it looked when Frederick Douglass was working there for the Aulds. Baltimore was a busy port, with ships sailing from there to everywhere in the world.

Boats filled the harbor and lined the wharves, where powerful men unloaded from them boxes and barrels of goods coming in from all over the world. Sailors rambled the streets looking for fun after their weeks at sea. Wagons, carts, and barrows rumbled along the docks. Always curious, always wanting to know what things were and how they worked, Frederick took it all in.

There was, too, the smell of freedom in the air. Baltimore was among the northernmost cities of the South. Fewer than fifty miles away was the border with Pennsylvania, a free state. Many escaping slaves passed through Baltimore on their way to freedom. In Baltimore, too, were a class of people Frederick had not seen much before—free blacks. Loose in the streets on errands, or looking after the Auld's boy, he was freer to wander around than he had ever been. He fell in with gangs of boys, many of them older, some of them white.

Ships being loaded in Baltimore. Although cranes were used to lift the heaviest loads, much of the work was done by hand. Many of the stevedores who did this kind of work were recent immigrants, especially from Ireland. This picture was probably painted somewhat after Frederick Douglass's time in Baltimore.

Hugh Auld left Frederick mainly to help his wife, Sophia, around the house. She was a religious person and sang hymns while she worked around the house. Every day she read from the Bible to her young son and Frederick. Frederick was intensely curious about this business of reading. Somehow, it seemed to him, Miss Sophia was taking words out of the book and speaking them. How was this magic done? He asked her. Sophia Auld, unaware that it was forbidden to teach slaves to read, decided that she would show Frederick how the mystery worked. Like her sister-in-law Lucretia, like Daniel Lloyd, she saw something in Frederick she wanted to encourage. He had an intelligence and curiosity that marked him as somehow different from ordinary boys, especially slaves. She began to show him words in the Bible. Soon he had learned the alphabet and was able to spell a few short words.

But then Sophia's husband, Hugh, learned about the reading lessons. He was very upset. "If you learn him how to read, he'll want to know how to write; and this accomplished, he'll be running away with himself." The reading lessons came to an end. As it turned out, Hugh Auld was absolutely right.

Once again a door had been opened, and Frederick was determined to march through it. He began asking the boys he knew on the streets to teach him how to spell this or that word.

In time, one of the boys gave him a spelling book. Frederick studied it every chance he got. By now the Auld's boy was going to school. He brought the day's lessons home with him at night. When nobody was around, Frederick would seize upon them and copy out words and sentences. Finally, when he was beginning to read fairly well, he bought with a carefully saved fifty cents a book called *The Columbian Orator*. It was a book of speeches and writings. Frederick studied them, reading them again and again, reciting them out loud. Some of the pieces in *The Columbian Orator* concerned human rights and liberties. Some were about slavery. Not only was Frederick learning to read from this book, he was learning a lot of the great ideas of important thinkers. His mind was awakening.

Chapter 3

THE SLAVEBREAKER

AND THEN SUDDENLY IT ALL STOPPED. In 1833, when Frederick was fifteen, the two Auld brothers quarreled. Frederick still officially belonged to Thomas Auld, who was living in the country on the Eastern Shore of Maryland, where Frederick had been born. Tom took Frederick back.

Slaves working in a rice paddy in Louisiana. Rice was grown in marshy land in a very hot climate. Slaves often sickened and died there from diseases like malaria. They all dreaded being sold off to the Deep South.

He was not the same boy who had left seven years earlier. He was now an adolescent, growing tall and strong. He had had a small taste of freedom. He had seen a bit of the larger world. He knew how to read a little. And perhaps most important, he had come to hate slavery from the bottom of his soul.

In his later writings Frederick said that hard feelings grew up between him and Thomas Auld because a horse he was caring for kept escaping. However, the real reason, certainly, was that Frederick had developed a new attitude: the sense that he was just as good a man as his master. He often answered back. He had become "impudent," and "uppity." Auld whipped him, and whipped him again. Finally he decided to send him out for a year to a man named Edward Covey.

This was a common practice. Many slaveholders had more slaves than they could use on their farms. They would rent the extra ones out to farmers who needed more help. Edward Covey was known to be a very hard master, who could usually tame unruly slaves. Slaveholders sometimes rented difficult slaves to Covey for low prices just to have their spirits broken. So, now Thomas sent Frederick to Covey.

Not long after arriving at his new home, Covey told Frederick to pick up a load of logs in the woods with a team of oxen and a cart. Frederick, who had been living in a city, was not used to driving oxen. All went well until they reached the woods. Here the oxen suddenly got frightened and began to run, the cart slamming and banging into trees. Finally the oxen got caught in a tree themselves. The cart tipped over, and the excited oxen soon had the harness thoroughly tangled in the cart and young trees.

In a panic Frederick struggled to set the cart upright. He cut down the young trees in which the harness was tangled, and finally managed to get the oxen under control. He loaded the cart and set out for home. But he was now very late.

The oxen behaved better on the return trip, until they saw the gates to the farm. As Frederick went to open the gate, the oxen suddenly charged forward, eager to get back into the barn. Frederick just had time to leap out of the way. The cart smashed against the gatepost, breaking the gate.

Covey, hearing the noise, suddenly appeared. He ordered Frederick back into the woods. Coming after him, he cut three switches from a gum tree. Then he ordered Frederick to take off his clothes. Frederick refused. Covey leapt at him, tore the clothes from him, and whipped Frederick until the three switches wore out.

It was only the first of many whippings. But as bad as the whippings were, the work was even worse. Covey kept his slaves hard at work from dawn until it was dark. Sometimes the slaves were kept in the fields until eleven or twelve at night, working by moonlight. Often Covey would set his slaves to work, and then go off as if leaving the farm for other business. Then he would slip quietly back, sometimes crawling through ditches, to spy on the slaves. Thus, even when Covey did not seem to be around, the slaves had to work hard for fear that he was secretly watching them.

One day in 1834 Frederick and some of the other slaves were working at separating grains of wheat from the straw stalks they grew on. It was August. The sun was blazing hot and there was no breeze. Frederick began to feel ill, probably from heatstroke. His strength drained away, his head ached, he grew dizzy. Suddenly he staggered and fell. The work stopped.

Covey now appeared, wondering what had happened. He saw Frederick lying in the dust and ordered him to stand. But Frederick was too weak to rise. Covey gave him a savage kick in the side. Once again Frederick tried to stand, but could not. Covey kicked him again. Frederick staggered to his feet and collapsed again. Covey snatched up a heavy board and cursing, smacked Frederick on the head. He turned to the other slaves to get the work going again.

Frederick lay in the dust, bleeding. After awhile he felt stronger. He staggered up and slipped away, determined to go home to Thomas Auld. Perhaps Auld would stop Covey from mistreating Frederick. He walked the seven miles to Auld's house, his face covered with blood. Auld, however, would not help him. Frederick must go back to Covey and finish out his year of service. In the morning he walked back to Covey's. As he approached the house, Covey spotted him and came after him with a whip.

Now Frederick fled into a field of corn, which was tall enough to hide him. From there he made his way to the home of a black man named Sandy, whose wife was free and had her own cabin. Sandy and his wife gave the hungry fugitive food and heard his story. Then Sandy told Frederick about a special root he knew of. If Frederick carried the root in his pocket, no white man would be able to whip him.

Frederick thought this was a silly idea; he had had some education and did not believe in such folktales. But Sandy insisted, and in order to please him, Frederick took the root and went back to Covey's farm.

The next day, Covey ordered Frederick to get down some feed for the horses from the barn loft. As Frederick was climbing the loft ladder, Covey slipped up behind him and grabbed Frederick's leg. He jerked him down to the stable floor and started to tie him up.

Frederick sprang to his feet. Suddenly a new feeling was on him. He was not going to let Covey lash him. He would fight. He grabbed Covey by the throat and began squeezing his neck. Now a real fight began. Several times Frederick was able to throw Covey to the ground. Covey shouted for help. His young cousin quickly appeared. Frederick smashed out at him. The young cousin staggered, but then grabbed for Frederick's hand, hoping to get a rope around his wrist. "I gave him a kick which sent him staggering away in pain."

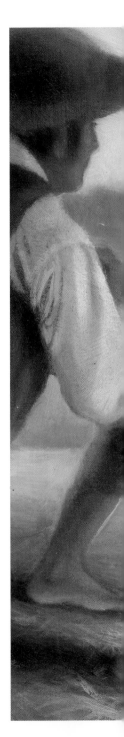

For two hours they fought. Several times Covey shouted to the other slaves to grab Frederick, but they would not. Finally Covey gave up. Letting Frederick go he said, "Now you scoundrel, go to your work. I would not have whipped you half so much as I have had you not resisted." Inwardly Frederick laughed, for Covey had not whipped him at all. And for the rest of his time at the farm, Covey never again laid a finger on Frederick.

The experience had been a critical one for Frederick. He wrote later that it was "the turning point in my life as a slave . . . I was a changed being after that fight. I was nothing before; I was a man now." He was even more determined to gain his freedom.

Readers may wonder why a slave so badly treated did not simply run away. The problem was this: not just the owner, but all other whites in the area would be on the lookout for a runaway slave. Sometimes a posse of whites with dogs would go looking for the runaway. Even whites who owned no slaves would help in tracking down runaways. They, too, believed that African Americans had to be kept down. Escaping, then, was difficult, and a slave who tried it was likely to be sold south, where escape was even more difficult.

According to the Fugitive Slave Act, runaway slaves had to be returned to their owners if caught, even in free states. Many Northerners were opposed to this law and tried to prevent runaways from being returned to slavery. As a result, the United States Army was sometimes used to return the slaves to their masters. In this picture some people in the crowd weep as two slaves caught in Boston are taken away by U.S. troops.

At the end of his year with Covey, Thomas Auld once again rented Frederick out, this time to a man named William Freeland. He was a much kinder master, who did not whip his slaves often and fed them well. The work was still hard and long, but conditions were much better at Freeland's place.

Moreover, Frederick found good friends at Freeland's. Among them were two brothers, John and Henry, who belonged to Freeland. Frederick became close to these two, as well as to some of the other slaves at Freeland's who were more or less his own age.

Slaves sometimes sang to lighten their work. Here, slaves sing as they shuck corn. In some cases there were special songs for each type of work.

As was usually the case with slaves, neither John nor Henry could read. Frederick now began explaining to them the importance of education—how being able to read had opened his eyes to the immorality and injustice of slavery. The brothers were willing to learn. They collected a few others, and Frederick began to teach them the alphabet and spelling on Sundays. They had, of course, to keep white people from knowing about this little school, so they met in the woods under the shade of a large oak tree.

Soon Frederick had twenty or thirty students. In bad weather they met in barns, and in winter at the cabin of a free black, at great risk to him. Later, after Frederick had become famous as a writer and lecturer, he said that with everything he had accomplished, nothing had given him more satisfaction than this little Sunday school. He had become, even as a teenager, a leader among blacks, trying to show them the way out of their misery.

But he was still a slave. The next year, 1835, Freeland decided he wanted to rent Frederick for another year. Now, Frederick told himself, it was time to plan his escape. As he thought about it later, he realized that under the horrors of Covey's rule, he had not thought of escaping. In such bad circumstances a person thinks only of getting from one day to the next without too much pain. But under better conditions, the idea of freedom has room to work in.

Frederick cautiously sounded out the brothers John and Henry about the idea of escaping. They agreed to it, and two others joined in the plot. For weeks they discussed the idea, looking at it from every angle.

There were many dangers. To begin with, their knowledge of the area was limited. They did not have maps available to them. They had only a hazy idea that the free states were somewhere to the north. How far they did not know. Beyond the free states there was Canada, but precisely where Canada was they did not know either.

Further, near the borders there were always slave catchers on the lookout for runaways: there was good money in catching a runaway slave, who might be worth $1,500, a great deal of money in those days.

Posters offering rewards for runaway slaves were commonplace in the South. Slaves were worth several hundred dollars, as the $100 reward being offered suggests.

$100 REWARD!

RANAWAY

From the undersigned, living on Current River, about twelve miles above Doniphan, in Ripley County, Mo., on 2nd of March, 1860, A NE GRO MAN, about 30 years old, weighs about 160 pounds; high forehead, with a scar on it; had on brown pants and coat very much worn, and an old black wool hat; shoes size No. 11.

The above reward will be given to any person who may apprehend this said negro out of the State; and fifty dollars if apprehended in this State outside of Ripley county, or $25 if taken in Ripley county.

But they would not give up. Eventually they came up with a plan. Freeland owned a large canoe. The plotters would slip away in the canoe some dark night and paddle as hard as they could up Chesapeake Bay. At the top of the bay they could go overland until they came to the border with Pennsylvania, a free state. (The border was only ten or fifteen miles above Chesapeake Bay, although they did not know that.) The Chesapeake could be rough in bad weather, but they would have to chance that.

Finally the great morning came. They went into the fields as usual. While working there Frederick had a sudden feeling, "which flashed upon me like lightning in a dark night." Somebody had given them away, he felt. Sure enough, a half hour later some constables arrived on horseback. Freeland called Frederick into the kitchen, saying that some gentlemen wished to speak to him. The "gentlemen" grabbed Frederick, and tied him up. They then collected the rest of the plotters, took them to a nearby town and shut them up in jail.

Outside the jail, slave traders gathered. Soon the plotters would be sold and these men wanted to get in on the deal. They were allowed in the prison to inspect Frederick and his friends, feeling their arms and legs to see how strong they were.

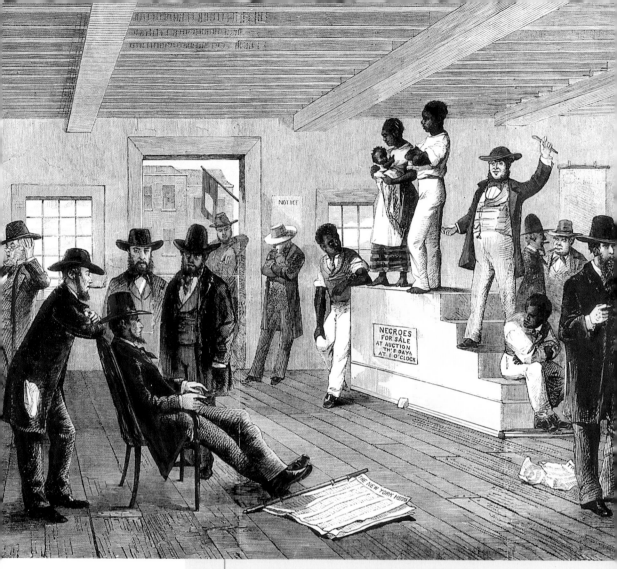

A slave auction in Virginia. Being auctioned off like cattle was a particularly humiliating experience for slaves. Sometimes potential buyers poked and prodded them to make sure they were strong and healthy.

Meanwhile, Thomas Auld was trying to decide what to do about Frederick. The plotters refused to admit that they had been planning to escape. The only evidence against them was the word of the person who had given them away. They had not, after all, been caught trying to escape. Nonetheless, Auld could easily believe that the impudent, independent-minded Frederick might well have been planning to run away. People told him that he ought to sell Frederick south.

But in the end, Thomas could not do it. Once again that special quality in Frederick did its work. Auld could not bring himself to sell Frederick to a short, hard life in the rice fields of Louisiana. On the other hand, he no longer wanted to deal with such an independent-minded slave himself. So he sent him back to his brother, Hugh Auld, in Baltimore. There Frederick would learn a trade. He could then be rented out and at least bring in a little money. So back to Baltimore Frederick went.

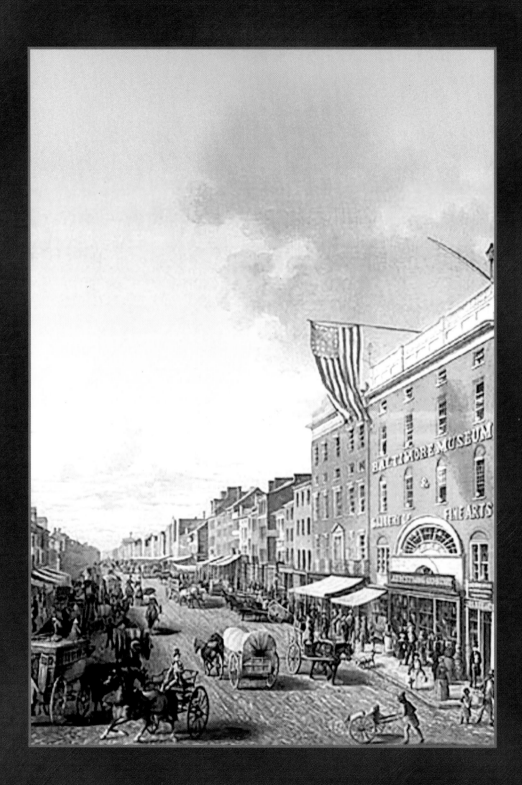

Chapter 4

FREEDOM AT LAST

FREDERICK BAILEY WAS NOW EIGHTEEN, a strong, handsome, and intelligent man, six feet tall, who could read and write better than many of the white people around him. He was determined to find freedom and a place in the larger world he felt destined for. But for that he needed money.

Baltimore a few years after Frederick Douglass lived there. It was a bustling, prosperous city at the time. Note the brick sidewalks and the unpaved street. The "museum" at right would actually have been a jumble of curiosities, like five-legged cows and skeletons of supposedly extinct animals.

As we have seen, Hugh Auld was in the shipbuilding business. He decided that Frederick would learn the trade of caulking. The sides of the ships of that day, no matter how small or large, were made of wooden planks. There was always a little space between the planks where water could seep through. To prevent such leaks, the cracks between the planks were packed with oakum—a fiber soaked with tar. The caulker laid the oakum along a crack, and pounded it into the crack with a chisel-like tool and a hammer.

At first, Hugh Auld had difficulty in getting a caulking job for Frederick: many of the shipyard workers did not want to work alongside blacks. But eventually Frederick started learning how to caulk. He soon mastered the trade; but of course his wages were being paid to Hugh Auld. Needless to say, Frederick resented that, and it made him more determined than ever to find freedom.

He needed a way to raise money for his escape, in any case. He knew that in Baltimore many slaves had made an arrangement with their masters whereby they found their own jobs, and supported themselves, in turn giving their masters so much money per week. Many masters liked this arrangement, for it meant that they collected some money every week, without having to take care of the slave.

Frederick made such an arrangement with Hugh Auld. He worked at caulking during the day, and in order to make extra money often worked at night, probably as a domestic servant. He began to save a little money. More free to come and go as he wanted than he had been, he began associating with the free African-American workmen of Baltimore. Among these people there was always talk about slavery—its evils, and how it could be ended. These free blacks, too, sometimes helped runaway slaves to pass through Baltimore on the way to a free state, at risk to themselves. Through them, Frederick was learning how to make his escape.

From Baltimore there were two main routes north. One went through New Jersey, up the Hudson River, across the Mohawk River to Lake Ontario and then Canada. The other went through New York City and then on up to New England. Especially in Massachusetts, there were many whites who were opposed to slavery and would help runaway blacks.

Runaway slaves were worth good money and were hunted relentlessly by their owners, posses of officials, and professional slave catchers. If caught, they were often sold south, where life for slaves was especially hard.

Meanwhile, Frederick had fallen in love. He was now twenty; it was time he thought about marriage. The woman was a free black named Anna Murray. She was five years older than Frederick, and had come from the Eastern Shore, not far from where Frederick had lived as a child. How she became free is not known. But when Frederick met her she was working as a domestic servant for a well-to-do Baltimore family. As a free black, she could leave Baltimore, but Frederick, of course, could not. They planned to marry and live in Baltimore at least until he could gain his freedom.

And then suddenly their plans were interrupted. One time Frederick was late in bringing his weekly payment to Hugh Auld. Auld was angry and decided to end the arrangement. Frederick would have to come back to live with the Aulds. Plans for the marriage would have to be put aside. Frederick had by now had a taste of freedom. He was not going to give it up. He and Anna decided he must escape now.

Hastily they made plans. To begin with, Frederick needed some kind of papers to show that he was not a runaway. Free blacks had what were called "free papers." Frederick tried to get false free papers, but could not. Instead, a free black sailor he knew offered him something almost as good. Sailors of any race carried seamen's papers, showing that they were qualified to work on ships. Slaves were not likely to have seamen's papers—it was too easy for a slave to board a ship going to free territory and thus escape. People would assume that any black who had seamen's papers was free.

It is probable that Frederick bought the seamen's papers from his sailor friend, although it is possible that the man gave them to him as a gift. Either way, it was a generous thing to do, for it left the sailor at risk until he replaced the seamen's papers.

Besides the papers, Frederick needed money to buy train and boat tickets and to keep him going for awhile if he succeeded in escaping. He had saved some money, but not enough. Anna Murray gave him some more.

On September 3, 1838, Frederick arose early in the morning. He dressed in a red shirt commonly worn by sailors, a kerchief around his neck in sailor fashion, and a sailor's broad, flat hat. Although Frederick had never been a sailor, he had for years worked in shipyards as a caulker and at other jobs. He said, "I knew a ship from stem to stern . . . and could talk sailor like an 'old salt.' "

With his seamen's papers in his pocket he got into a horse-drawn cab owned by a friend of his. Frederick did not want to buy a ticket at the railroad station, where his papers might be carefully examined. Instead, the cabbie waited until the last minute. Then he raced up to the station as the train was getting ready to leave. He pulled up to the car assigned to blacks—he knew exactly where it would be. Frederick leaped aboard. The train whistle screamed, the wheels began to turn, and the adventure had begun.

It took a long time for the conductor to make his way through the train collecting tickets. The train was almost at the last stop in Maryland when he got to Frederick. His heart was beating so fast and loud he thought that the conductor must be able to hear it. The conductor said, "I suppose you have your free papers?"

"No, Sir; I never carry my free papers to sea with me," Frederick replied as casually as he could. He pulled out the seamen's papers, which had an American eagle at the top and looked very official—as indeed they were. The problem was that the sailor described in them in no way resembled

Frederick. But the conductor was in a rush. He glanced at the papers, sold Frederick his ticket, and turned to the next passenger. Relief swept Frederick, and his heart began to slow down.

But the dangers were not over. Now he had to take a ferry across the Susquehanna River to Delaware. Here he ran into a deckhand whom he knew from Baltimore. The deckhand, curious at seeing Frederick so far from home, asked him where he was going. In sudden fear, Frederick made a quick excuse and went off to the other end of the ferry, praying that the deckhand wouldn't say something that would give him away.

Once across the river, Frederick walked quickly down the ramp and got onto a train heading north. There was a south-bound train standing on the next track. Frederick glanced at it. Sitting in a window looking directly at him was a ship captain he had often seen around the shipyard where he had worked. The captain was staring directly at Frederick, but didn't notice who he was. Frederick turned his head away. In doing so he saw another man staring at him from the south-bound train. Frederick knew him well. He was a German blacksmith whom he had also worked with. The blacksmith, Frederick was sure, recognized him. "I really believe he knew me, but had no heart to betray me."

To Frederick's relief the train soon pulled away, chugging toward Wilmington. Here Frederick made his way to a ferry, clambered aboard, and went up the river to Philadelphia. He was now in a free state, but he knew he could not linger, because there were many slave catchers in the city. He went immediately to a ferry, crossed over to the New Jersey side, and boarded a night train going north. The next morning, September 4, he took a ferry across the Hudson River to Manhattan. When he got off that ferry he felt free at last.

Standing amid the "hurrying throngs" and "dazzling wonders of Broadway," he was filled with "sensations . . . too intense and too rapid for words." He said, "All of the dreams of my childhood and the purposes of my manhood were now fulfilled . . . what a moment this was to me."

In New York City he sent for Anna. She arrived wearing a new plum-colored silk dress. He had brought with him a suit carefully packed in his seaman's bag. Wearing their new clothes, they were married by another runaway who had become a minister.

They knew they could not stay in New York—there were too many slave catchers there. They were advised by friends that they ought to go north to New Bedford, Massachusetts, a city on the Atlantic Coast. New Bedford was one of the most prosperous small cities in the United States. Its wealth came mainly from whaling. At the time, much home lighting came from oil lamps. Whale oil was one of the main types of fuel used for these lamps. The demand for it was great. Shipyards in New Bedford were busy building the whaling boats used in that dangerous trade. From the port sailed not just whaling vessels but ships bound everywhere in the world.

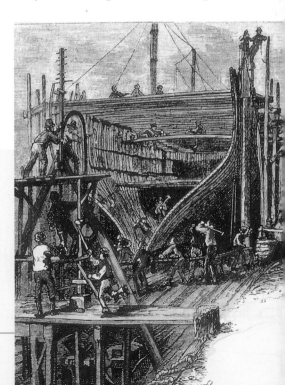

Shipbuilding was a major industry in New England and employed many workers. The United States was rapidly becoming one of the world's great marine powers.

Furthermore, many people in Massachusetts, particularly in New Bedford, were opposed to slavery. Slave catchers were not welcome there. They risked being mobbed if they tried to capture a runaway and haul him back south. So the newly married couple took a boat from New York through Long Island Sound to New Bedford.

Frederick could not of course use his real name, for fear of the Aulds coming after him. In New York he had taken the name of Frederick Johnson, but when he got to New Bedford he discovered many blacks named Johnson. To avoid confusion, he sought another name. A friend suggested one from a popular story about Scottish rebels. Frederick liked the bravery of the Scots in throwing off their rulers. One of the rebel leaders was named Douglass. He now became Frederick Douglass. It would soon be one of the best-known names in the United States. (The spelling with two *s*s was common at the time.)

Less happily, Frederick was discovering that the North was by no means free of dislike for blacks. As in the South, most people in the North believed that African Americans were naturally inferior to whites—not as intelligent, sensible, or sensitive as whites. Many thought that blacks could not really take care of themselves, and needed whites to rule over them. Such people did not wish to associate with blacks. In most cases blacks were forced to sit in separate railroad cars. They could not easily get tables at restaurants or rooms in hotels. Many white parents did not want their children going to school with blacks. In most Northern places blacks were not allowed to vote. Nor would most white families welcome blacks into their homes except as servants.

Nonetheless, Frederick had to work. He went to a boatyard hoping to get a job as a caulker, which he was now very good at doing. The boss of the yard told him flatly, "Every white man would leave the ship . . . unfinished . . . if I struck a blow at my trade upon her." Part of the problem, as it had been in Baltimore, was that white workers feared that blacks would work for lower wages and would take the whites' jobs. But much of it was simple dislike of working alongside "inferior" people. Frederick was forced to take lower-paying work cutting wood, shoveling coal, unloading ships, scrubbing ship cabins—the hardest and least rewarding kind of work.

A whaling ship tipped on one side for repairs. Douglass tried to get a job in a shipyard like this one but was turned down because white workers did not want black ones competing for their jobs.

Nonetheless, he was happy to be free, despite everything, and able to keep all of his wages for himself. He and Anna found a small house and started raising a family.

Hostility toward blacks, however, came not just from laboring men. Frederick at first joined a mainly white church. He was required to sit in the upstairs gallery. He soon noticed that the white worshipers were allowed to take the sacraments first while the blacks had to stand aside and wait. This was too much for Frederick, and he joined a black church.

In the colonial days blacks and whites usually went to the same churches, with blacks sitting in the balconies. By about 1800 blacks were starting their own churches to avoid being treated as second-class citizens in white churches. This picture shows a church in Washington, D.C., at the time Douglass was living there.

But there was another, more friendly face to the North. Going well back into the colonial period, there had always been a small group of Northerners opposed to slavery. This was especially true in New England, which had always had a strong religious bent. By Frederick Douglass's time a powerful abolitionist movement had developed. People were publishing newspapers about the evils of slavery, making speeches on the subject, raising money to help slaves escape. Many of the abolitionists did not really want equality for African Americans, but they felt that it was un-Christian and immoral to keep human beings in slavery. The opinion of such people was that conditions for blacks ought to be improved, but that did not mean they should mingle socially. Others, however, did believe in equality for blacks and were willing to fight for it.

By the time of Frederick's escape to New Bedford, the most important of the abolitionist leaders was a white man named William Lloyd Garrison. He was a vigorous speaker and published a newspaper favoring abolition called *The Liberator*. He would soon come into Frederick's life.

William Lloyd Garrison was perhaps the most important abolitionist of his time. He sponsored Douglass and got him started as a lecturer. Douglass was always grateful to Garrison but came to feel that Garrison and his friends wanted to manage him, while he wanted to make his own decisions about his work. Eventually he went his own way.

The masthead of Garrison's famous antislavery newspaper. The color is not original, but was added later.

At a church meeting in March 1839 the subject of slavery came up. Frederick rose and told the others what slavery was really like. Word of this brief speech reached William Lloyd Garrison, and he printed a little story about it in *The Liberator*. Frederick was startled and excited. He had been a regular reader of the *The Liberator*. He said, "I loved this paper and its editor. . . . His words were few, full of holy fire, and straight to the point." To be noticed by Garrison seemed like a great honor to Frederick.

Now, increasingly, Frederick became determined to fight slavery any way that he could. It was not enough to have escaped bondage himself; he had to help others to do so. He began to attend the meetings and lectures held by various abolitionist groups.

At one of these meetings someone remembered the little talk he had given on slavery at the church meeting. He suggested that Frederick tell his own story. Frederick stood and told some of the stories we have been reading about—the fight with Covey, the whippings, the escape. His audience was enthralled. Frederick was beginning to see that he had a calling. He had always sensed that he had something special to say and do. It was now clear what that special task was.

He began speaking more frequently at meetings, usually telling the story of his bondage and escape. In 1841 at one such meeting, in the audience was a well-known abolitionist from the island of Nantucket, not far from New Bedford. He was impressed by this handsome, well-spoken, determined young man. It was surprising to him, as to many others, that this black man with no schooling, so recently a slave, spoke so well and fluently, as if he had had a college education. He asked Frederick to come to Nantucket to speak.

Word was beginning to get around about this runaway slave who spoke so beautifully and passionately. A number of important abolitionist leaders decided to come to Nantucket to hear Frederick's speech. A little awed by them, at first Frederick was unsure of himself and spoke quietly. But soon he was warmed by his own words. The phrases began to roll out, his voice grew strong and resonant. One man who heard this speech talked later about Frederick Douglass's "intellectual power," and his "wisdom as well as wit."

The audience was swept up, and roared when he was finished. At that point Garrison jumped to his feet, and cried, "Have we been listening to a thing . . . or a man?" (A slave who could be bought and sold was treated like a "thing.")

"A man, a man," the crowd shouted back.

"Shall such a man ever be sent back to bondage from the free soil of Massachusetts?" Garrison shouted.

"No, no, no," the crowd cried out.

At that moment, says one of his biographers, "Frederick knew a triumph so intense, so total, that he would spend his entire life seeking to sustain it."

Chapter 5

A DEDICATED LIFE

FREDERICK DOUGLASS'S LIFE WAS SUDDENLY changed. Garrison and other abolitionist leaders immediately realized that he was exactly the sort of speaker that they wanted. His speeches, they were sure, would convince many people of the evils of slavery and bring them into the abolitionist cause. It was not just that Douglass was a fascinating speaker with an incredible story to tell. It was that his intelligence, good manners, seriousness, and great skill with words demonstrated that African Americans could be the equal of whites.

A photograph of Frederick Douglass when he was about thirty and busy telling the story of his life as a slave and his escape to enthralled audiences.

Garrison quickly signed Douglass up as a regular speaker for his organization, the Massachusetts Anti-Slavery Society. For the first time in his life, Frederick Douglass had a regular salary. It was not a large one, that is true, but it was enough to allow him, Anna, and the children to live comfortably. The society helped to buy him a small house in Lynn, which was closer to the headquarters in Boston than New Bedford was.

We must realize that in a day when there was no television, radio, or movies, going to lectures was an important activity for Americans. A lecture was expected to be educational, but it must also be interesting. People thought nothing of listening to a talk for two or three hours at a stretch. A popular lecturer could tour from city to city around the country for months at a time, giving lectures almost every night. The most popular of them made a great deal of money from their lectures.

Douglass could not make a lot of money from his talks. The money earned from them went to the abolitionist cause. But he was certainly a wonderful speaker, always in demand. One reporter who heard him speak said, "No printed sentence can convey any adequate idea of the manner, the tone of voice, the gesticulation, the action, the round, soft, swelling pronunciation with which Frederick Douglass spoke." He was a natural storyteller, with dramatic and horrifying stories to tell. He was, in fact, one of the greatest American lecturers of his day.

He was also one of the best writers. In 1845 he wrote the story of his days in slavery, which was called *Narrative of the Life of Frederick Douglass, an American Slave. Written by Himself.* The book was an instant success. Says one writer, with the publishing of that book Douglass "became, almost overnight, the most celebrated black author in history." This book and two others he wrote about his life are classics and still widely read.

In 1845 Douglass published his story in a short book. It created a sensation, not just because of the terrible tale it had to tell, but because it showed that a black born into slavery could learn to write more effectively than most whites. Many people, even in the North, did not believe that a black person could be that smart.

NARRATIVE

OF THE

LIFE

OF

FREDERICK DOUGLASS,

AN

AMERICAN SLAVE.

WRITTEN BY HIMSELF.

BOSTON:
PUBLISHED AT THE ANTI-SLAVERY OFFICE,
No. 25 CORNHILL.
1845.

By 1850 the abolitionists were beginning to win their battles. Ever larger numbers of people in the North were coming to believe that slavery had to be ended. In turn, Southerners, feeling their way of life threatened, were digging in their heels—their slaves must not be taken from them. People could see that a split was coming. Frantically, politicians from both sides looked for compromises, but neither the abolitionists in the North, nor the people in the South were willing to compromise very much—even though the majority of Southerners actually owned no slaves.

Another important abolitionist, Wendell Phillips, on the lecture platform. Going to lectures was not only educational for Americans at the time, but a source of entertainment. A good lecturer had to move his or her audience.

William Lloyd Garrison and some of the other abolitionists were pleased by the intensity of the fight. They felt that there should be no compromise: if the South wanted to break away from the Union, let them.

At first Frederick accepted the leadership of Garrison, whom he so much admired. But as time went on, he began having second thoughts. For one thing, if the South broke away, the North would no longer have any power to end slavery there. Douglass was coming to believe that it would be best to try to find a political solution to the problem of slavery. Did not the Declaration of Independence say flatly that "all men are created equal"? The United States was based on that idea. Therefore, in time Americans must be persuaded that blacks had to be given the same rights as whites.

Garrison did not agree. He felt that because the Constitution did not forbid slavery, it was an immoral document and should be ignored. Douglass and Garrison were seeing things differently.

Frederick Douglass giving a lecture. He was a masterful speaker who often left his audience in tears.

There was another point, as well. Douglass was getting the feeling that Garrison and the other white abolitionists wanted him merely to do the lecturing, and let them set policy. He was starting to feel that they saw him as their puppet. He did not like that idea. He was, he thought, quite capable of thinking for himself. He decided he could no longer follow Garrison's policies. Instead, he would start his own magazine in which he would set forth his opinions. Garrison and the others protested, for it was hard enough to raise money to keep *The Liberator* going: they did not need a competing magazine. But Douglass was determined. He called his paper the *North Star*, for the star that guided slaves to freedom.

He now turned to politics. He worked for the election of people who would fight against slavery. When the new Republican party was formed in the 1850s with an antislavery policy, he supported it. Very quickly, Douglass became the most important African-American political figure in the country. He often met with presidents, senators, and other officials to discuss problems of blacks. Eventually he was named ambassador to Haiti, the first nation in the Western Hemisphere run by blacks.

At the time some of the abolitionists said that Douglass had become proud and vain. It is certainly true that Douglass had that sense of his own specialness. It is also true that he had a weakness for honors. He felt it was owed to him that he should meet presidents, be given important political jobs—although in fact he got few of these. But in truth, Douglass was entitled to a little vanity. After all, he had achieved far more than most people after starting from the very bottom of the heap.

Yet despite his fame as a writer, lecturer, and editor, the battle against racism was never ending. Once, when he was speaking on an open-air platform in Indiana, some thugs jumped onto the stand and began to pull it apart. Two of Douglass's friends gathered around him to protect him. Douglass saw another of his associates in danger. He grabbed up a piece of lumber. Some of the thugs began shouting, "Kill the nigger." Douglass started to run. The thugs chased him, knocked him down, and broke his right hand. They might have killed him if some of his friends had not come up in time.

Prejudice against blacks was great. Many Americans with little education grew angry when confronted by an African American with great skill in writing and speaking, and sometimes they started trouble. Douglass on occasion had to defend himself against attacks.

This was one of the worst incidents Douglass faced, but there were others. Many times eggs, and even stones, were thrown at him. A fine house that he had built for his family was burned to the ground. But nothing would deter him; he would carry his message about the evils of slavery to the end.

In 1860 Abraham Lincoln was elected president. His goal, he said, was not to end slavery, but to keep the United States from splitting apart. The South did not believe him, and at the end of 1860 the Southern states began to secede, or withdraw, from the Union. Soon they formed their own country, which they called the Confederate States of America. And in April 1861 the terrible Civil War began.

At first, Lincoln continued to insist that the war was not about slavery, but about preserving the Union. However, over time his opinion changed. He saw that if the North won and brought the Southern states back into the Union, slavery would have to end. He therefore issued the famous Emancipation Proclamation, freeing the slaves. Of course the blacks held in the South were still slaves, until the war ended. But with the victory of the North, slavery was over.

A scene in Washington, D.C., showing blacks celebrating their newfound freedom after the Civil War.

Frederick Douglass was not alone in bringing an end to slavery in America. Millions of people helped, including about 360,000 Northern whites who died in the Civil War to help slaves become free. But Douglass was a very important voice in showing Americans the evils of slavery and convincing them that slavery was truly immoral.

Unfortunately, although slavery was ended, inequality was not, and would not be for a long time. In the North, prejudice against blacks remained. It was still hard for them to get good jobs, hard for them to be seated in restaurants or get rooms in hotels. It was even harder for them to run for public office or get appointments to government offices.

Resentment of blacks remained strong in the South after they gained their freedom. Whites particularly disliked seeing blacks getting educated. Here, whites burn down a school for blacks started after the war by the U.S. government.

In the South matters were even worse. Whites there were determined to push blacks into serfdom, a condition little better than slavery. They threatened, then beat blacks who demanded fair treatment. Blacks who tried to vote were turned away from the voting booths on flimsy excuses. Any black who tried to rise in the world was in danger. By the end of the nineteenth century, when Frederick Douglass was growing old, there came a wave of lynchings across the South. Blacks who did not know their place were accused of terrible crimes like rape and murder, which in most cases they did not commit. Instead of getting a fair trial, they would be dragged from their cabins and hung from a tree or a lamppost while a crowd of whites cheered. Some were burnt alive. The lynchings of the late nineteenth and early twentieth centuries were part of a shameful time in American history.

Frederick Douglass spoke out against lynchings and the inequalities blacks faced everywhere. But neither the government nor the American people as a whole was listening. The United States was not ready for racial equality. Not until well into the twentieth century would racial walls begin to crumble.

But Frederick Douglass had achieved much in his lifetime. When he died in 1895 he was owner of a fine home with a view of the Capitol in Washington, D.C. He had been a friend of many presidents, a well-known figure in politics. No slave had ever risen as far as he had.

More important, through his lecturing and writing, he had been a major voice—perhaps the most important one—in awakening the conscience of America.

The elderly Frederick Douglass, now famous and well-to-do, shown with his grandson, Joseph. There still remained great barriers for African Americans in the United States, but much progress had been made.

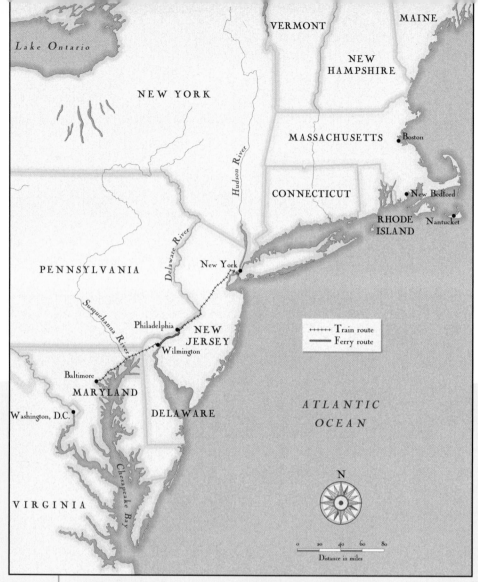

Lake Ontario

VERMONT   MAINE

NEW YORK

NEW
HAMPSHIRE

MASSACHUSETTS •Boston

Hudson River

CONNECTICUT   •New Bedford

RHODE
ISLAND   •Nantucket

Delaware River

PENNSYLVANIA

New York•

Susquehanna River

Philadelphia•

NEW
JERSEY

Wilmington•

Baltimore•

MARYLAND

DELAWARE

+++++ Train route
——— Ferry route

Washington, D.C.•

ATLANTIC
OCEAN

VIRGINIA

Chesapeake Bay

N

0   20   40   60   80
Distance in miles

*This map shows the route that Frederick Douglass took to
escape from slavery. From New York, he soon went on to
New Bedford, an important whaling port of the day.
Nantucket, where Douglass made the speech that brought
him to the attention of the abolitionists, was also a major
whaling center. After he began working in the abolitionist
cause, he moved his family to Lynn, about fifteen miles
north of Boston, to be closer to abolitionist headquarters.*

AUTHOR'S NOTE ON SOURCES

The best source for the life of Douglass is his own writing, especially the three autobiographies that he published. There is a one-volume edition of all three entitled *Frederick Douglass Autobiographies* published by the Library of America. There are also several inexpensive paperback editions of the first of the autobiograhies called *Narrative of the Life of Frederick Douglass*, which can be read by older students. For younger students, there is Frederick Douglass, by Sharman Apt Russell, and *Frederick Douglass and the Fight for Freedom*, by Douglas T. Miller.

McFeely, William S. *Frederick Douglass*. New York: W.W. Norton, 1991.

Miller, Douglas T. *Frederick Douglass and the Fight for Freedom*. New York: Facts on File, 1988. (young readers)

Russell, Sharman Apt. *Frederick Douglass*. New York: Chelsea House Publishers, 1988. (young readers)

INDEX

ABOUT THE AUTHOR

James Lincoln Collier has written many books, both fiction and nonfiction, for children and adults. His interests span history, biography, and historical fiction. He is an authority on the history of jazz and performs weekly on the trombone in New York City.

My Brother Sam Is Dead was named a Newbery Honor Book and a Jane Addams Honor Book and was a finalist for a National Book Award. *Jump Ship to Freedom* and *War Comes to Willy Freemen* were each named a notable Children's Trade Book in the Field of Social Studies by the National Council for Social Studies and the Children's Book Council. Collier received the Christopher Award for *Decision in Philadelphia: The Constitutional Convention of 1787*. He lives in Pawling, New York.